I0829039

This copy is presented to

with the compliments of the Committee, in the hope that the interest in a paramount social problem of New York will induce careful reading of the argument.

RAPID TRANSIT:

ITS EFFECT ON RENTS AND LIVING CONDITIONS AND HOW TO GET IT

BY

JOHN MARTIN

ADDRESSED TO RENT-PAYERS, SOCIAL WORKERS AND CITY STATESMEN

PUBLISHED AND SOLD BY
THE COMMITTEE ON CONGESTION OF POPULATION
165 BROADWAY
NEW YORK
March 1909

RAPID TRANSIT

ITS EFFECT ON RENTS AND LIVING CONDITIONS AND HOW TO GET IT

Rapid transit is at present one of the most important social problems in New York, a problem of humanity more than of money. It is the only amelioration in sight of the rent problem. Chief among city evils, parent of a brood of other evils, is high tenement rents. From high rents come congestion of population, overcrowding of rooms, and underfeeding. These in turn mean bad air and insufficient sunshine with low vitality, ill-health and tuberculosis in their train. High rents mean high land values and consequently meagre parks and crowded school-houses without playgrounds.

Without Rapid Transit the tenement districts must be crowded worse and worse, the rents mount higher and higher and the fight for decent conditions and against the Great White Plague be hopeless.

Small parks, playgrounds, tenement laws, medical inspection of school children, public baths, hospitals, dispensaries and the like, good as they are, can never bring health and humane environment so long as ever greater multitudes must swarm into districts already congested and ever a bigger part of family wages must go for shelter.

Rents To-day.

Already rents and the consequent ills in New York are appalling. Among decent, self-supporting families, of normal size, with an income of less than $600 a year, throughout Manhattan, an average of 26 per cent to 27 per cent of the family expenditure is for rent.* In the worst regions the proportionate levy is higher. In a block bounded by Allen, Stanton, Orchard, and Rivington streets** the families pay out thirty per cent of their income for their living "compartment," while the poorest families pay occasionally the bankrupting proportion of nearly half of all they get.

---

* These and many of the facts given on future pages are taken from the Report of an Investigation conducted by a special committee of the New York State Conference of Charities and Corrections. Published with numerous statistical tables and minute scientific evidence by the Sage Foundation, 105 East 22nd St., New York City.

** Examination of this block was made by Dr. Chas. S. Bernheimer, assistant head-worker of the University Settlement.

Even for these sacrificial sums they do not secure enough space, light and air for humanizing life. Overcrowding that is indecent and brutal is the rule in families with less than $800 a year. Among the self-sustaining, respectable wage-earners on Manhattan, of this grade, only about one in three can afford four rooms for himself, wife and children and over half have less than two rooms for every three persons.

When higher-priced tenements are occupied lodgers must be taken to help to pay the rent for the extra space. Over half of the more fortunate families, those that can pay over $14 a month rent, have a stranger in the household; and it is one of life's little ironies that among the families most overcrowded the lodger is most common. "From those that have not shall be taken away even that they have."

Overcrowding.

Among the poorest immigrants conditions are unimaginably bad. In an Italian quarter 52.4 per cent of the families live in one or two-room flats and most of them take in lodgers, so that many of the rooms "house" four and five persons.* Of a number of typical families recently examined by Settlement workers, families not dependent on charity, but living under normal conditions, 49 per cent were found crowded like rabbits with four or more to each room. And this in a Christian city of the twentieth century! With such bestial conditions, not mitigated, as they were in the old country, by life in the open air and the free circulation of the winds around the dwelling, no wonder that, in special blocks, the death rate is one-third higher than for the city as a whole, so that a quarter of all the people who die in these blocks are slaughtered by the foul overcrowding, and conditions that go with it.

New York is proving the force of Rousseau's words: "Men were not made to be massed together in herds. The more they herd together the more they corrupt one another. Infirmities of the body as well as evils of the soul are the inevitable effect of this over-accumulation. The breath of man is fatal to his fellows; that is no less true literally than figuratively."

---

* These conditions were revealed by an investigation conducted by the Committee on Congestion of Population at the expense of the Italian government.

In rich American households the bath-room, more important now-a-days than the nursery, is better equipped and more common than anywhere else in the world; but in the tenements, where large families make the bath-room most requisite, this aid to civilization is almost unknown. High rents put it beyond the reach of the plain people. That a bath-tub does not go with a one or two-room flat is part of "what every woman knows"; but few women know that to three-quarters of all the families earning less than the high rate of $1,100 a year the bath-room in New York is wanting.

Starve to Pay the Rent.

Still worse. To pay the rents even for their packing-box accommodations many families are starving themselves. According to the most careful, painstaking and scientific investigation ever made of living conditions in our city, all the full-sized families with less than $600 a year are underfed and of those wth $600 to $800 a year one in every three is underfed. And notice this most significant fact: "A comparison of nationalities suggests that the families which spend the largest proportion of their income for food are those which pay the smallest share of it for rent."* What a brutal alternative! Either crowd like pigs or starve like savages!

In brief, although the laboring man in New York is paying more for rent than he can afford, a bigger share of his income than in any part of any other city known, though he is actually going without food to get shelter, yet he is housed in such narrow, stifling quarters as makes family decency and the rearing of good citizens well nigh impossible.

Only a public enemy would aggravate such a shameful condition by obstructing Rapid Transit to undeveloped districts.

Unless Rapid transit is developed so as to bring wider areas into actual use tenement rents, staggering as they are to-day, will surely climb still higher. During 1908 there was a lull; but reviving business is bound to bring more immigrants and fresh troops from the rural districts, with keener demand for rooms and a repetition of past experience, periodical rent increases. In its report for 1905-6 the Charity Organization Society stated that "the most striking phenomenon of the past year in the experience of charitable agencies in New York

* Report of the Standard of Living of Workingmen's Families in New York City—page 123. The Russell Sage Foundation.

is the persistent increase in the rent of tenements." Every increase means either starvation or worse overcrowding.

Therefore Rapid Transit is not chiefly a financial problem; it is a social problem. It is a question, not of dollars, but of human lives. Delay will cost tenement dwellers millions in higher rents and incalculable loss of health, self-respect and humane development.

No Subway. Then Rent Increases Equal Cost of One.

Of New York's population at least a million and a half will have their rents affected by a dearth of Rapid Transit facilities. That means at least 300,000 families. Judging by rent increases in 1906 it is fair to assume that an average increase of 75c. a month will be made so soon as the flood-tide of population again rises. **Thereupon those families will be paying $2,700,000 a year additional rent, a 5 per cent return on $54,000,000, enough to build a subway. Clearly whether or not a subway be built it will be paid for**—paid for either by those who use it to get to more airy homes, or, cruel injustice, by those who, cribbed, cabin'd and confined, in quarters where they are huddled like galley-slaves below decks, must pay as much extra to remain as would provide means of escape. If it is not built the added rents will be capitalized, innocent investors will purchase the new "equity," converting it into a "vested interest," and any subsequent reduction of rents, if ever attainable, will be given the appearance of a confiscation of the property of the last purchaser.

Two million seven hundred thousand dollars a year! All the Settlements and relief agencies put together cannot make up to tenement-dwellers for this additional subsidy. Which is the more humane and sensible? To let rents rise and then try to relieve destitute families by paying their rent and giving them food or to keep down rents and foster family life by rapid transit in all directions?

Already the current of population outwards over the bridges and through the subway has washed out a few black civic stains. In the outlying boroughs less than half as many families are overcrowded, on the same income, as in Manhattan, while twice as many of them enjoy the comfort of a bath-room and private toilet. On the whole, then, twice as many children, proportionately, are being raised in decent conditions, favorable to family life, in Brooklyn, Queens, and the Bronx as in Manhattan. Civilization calls for the social, the municipal encouragement of a tendency which shows such humanizing results, a tendency that will increase in proportion as facilities for express transportation are improved.

Tuberculosis.

Our city is awake to the horrors of tuberculosis, the enemy that is striking to death ten thousand of its inhabitants every year, and New York has leaped honorably into the front rank among the cities fighting for the extermination of the modern plague. Doctors agree that the effective enemies of the detestable little germ are sunlight and fresh air. Without them the patient's fight against his tireless foe is hopeless; with them he stands a good chance to win. Therefore these maxims are essential items in every genuine recipe for consumption cure: "One place you can control. Your bed-room. Ventilate that." "Work in fresh air. Live in fresh air. Sleep in fresh air." But it is mockery to tell a family that is crowded with two, three, and four persons in every room—rooms not much bigger than a crate—to "live in fresh air" and to "ventilate the bed-room." As well tell them to buy new lungs. Fresh air and sunlight can't be got where high tenements, narrow streets, and crowded chambers mean that over a thousand souls swarm on every acre. Tuberculosis can never be conquered if population in the region below Fourteenth Street is to pile up each five years an additional eighty thousand as it did the last five years, and as it must do again unless lines of fast passage are immediately multiplied. Small parks, pitiful little breathing places, costly as they are, can only be a trifling mitigation of the evil; their effect cannot reach inside the dwellings. But out on the borders of Greater New York wide spaces, league after league, await occupation, spaces where the winds blow and the sun shines, spaces where cheap and healthy houses could be built with those best of therapeutic agents, through ventilation and real daylight in every room. To-day these spaces are unavailable because inaccessible; but subways and elevated lines could put them within half an hour of City Hall.

Therefore Rapid Transit is an ally the city must have in the campaign against the Great White Plague.

Transit Must be Cheap and Rapid.

To fulfill its social purposes transit must be of the cheapest and the most rapid. The workman whose push-cart, fruit-stand, shop or factory is in the city has neither time for a slow trip nor money for high fares. A nickel fare means $2.50 a month for him and another dollar a month or so for an occasional trip for wife and "kids." That is the maximum he can afford. Make the fare a dime and at once you put up a barrier of about ninety dollars a year, a seventh of his earnings, or thereabouts, against his removal from his Manhattan tenement.

Also the lower the condition of the laborer the longer the hours he works, and the more imperative his need for the fastest locomotion possible. Time to him is not only money; it is sleep and leisure. He cannot work ten to twelve hours a day and spend more than an hour each way between home and shop besides. He must take the dread alternative of a stuffy, high-priced tenement near his work.

So that the paramount problem which challenges the statesmanship and philanthropy of New York to-day is: How can lines of rapid transit be quickly multiplied under the condition which is as unalterable as the laws of the Medes and Persians—a maximum fare of five cents?

How to Finance Subways.

Subways can be financed by corporation money, by city money or by a combination of the two. The Hudson Companies' system of tunnels is financed by corporation money and the Brooklyn-Bronx system by a combination of city money for construction and corporation money for equipment.

Essential Conditions.

A few facts dissipate the expectation that private capital will build lines except on condition that either:

1. Fares are higher than a nickel, or
2. The lines shall run only through crowded sections and give short hauls.

Either of these conditions would be fatal to the prime social purpose of rapid transit, the relief of congestion of population by bringing cheap, vacant land into use.

The Brooklyn-Bronx subway was built on city credit and is operated on a fifty-year lease, tax free; and nobody expects a change of the law to offer more tempting conditions to private corporations. It is packed to suffocation and taps the richest traffic districts. Yet dividends on it, even though private capital provided only equipment, are paid by neglecting to provide either a depreciation fund on the equipment, which, says the Chamber of Commerce, "will undoubtedly have to be renewed perhaps more than once during the life of the contract," or a reserve to meet possible damage claims from accidents or, lastly, a fund to amortize the private capital invested in the Brooklyn extension, power houses, and so forth. Consequently, as the expert of the Public Service Commission says: "There will come a time when renewals must be made either at the expense of the stockholders or at the sacrifice of the service." Since the Public Service Commission is empowered to prevent "sacrifice of the service" this policy of saving nothing against the rainy day which is seen approaching can but result in "renewals at the expense of the stockholders," as is happening on the Manhattan surface lines, a prospect not likely to encourage investment in other subways under private financiering.

The Economy of City Money.

That subways similar to the Manhattan-Bronx line, which will carry passengers for five cents to districts sparsely settled, cannot be self-supporting unless every possible economy be practised has been conclusively demonstrated by Mr. Bion J. Arnold, special consulting engineer of the Public Service Commission. The most important savings, he shows, can be made on "Fixed charges"—interest on permanent way, and equipment, and sinking fund on permanent way—and he therefore recommends that, for future lines, not less but more city credit be used, by employing it to provide for equipment as well as permanent way. He shows that, while the city pays but 4 per cent for money, a private corporation must pay 6 per cent "as this is about as low as money usually costs a private corporation after paying brokerage and other expenses incidental to securing it." His words are corroborated by the experience of the Hudson Companies which are paying 6 per cent for loans to-day, although their tunnels, giving only short hauls and connecting crowded traffic centers, should offer an investment specially secure. Therefore the use of city money will save $1,500,000 a year on a new subway, a sum which passengers must furnish as an extra subsidy if the profligate method of private financing be adopted.

Summing up the most expert and thorough investigation of the whole problem ever made, this engineer, selected from the whole nation for his ability and experience, says:

"With the return upon the investment required by private capital there is now no field in New York for the construction of a comprehensive system of subways entirely with private capital unless the fare for the long-haul passenger is something more than the present five-cent fare."

This conclusion is confirmed by the Special Committee on Rapid Transit of the Chamber of Commerce,* which reports that "it has become apparent that the financial problem (involved in future subway construction) is beset by so many uncertainties that private capital cannot look upon the undertaking as a safe business venture." To cure this defect and "make the undertaking a safe business venture," a few concessions, says this committee, would need to be made by a generous public.

1. Ten cent fares on express trains must be allowed, about which "the public must be informed and public opinion developed."

2. Pipe galleries should not be required in subways and advertising in cars and stations should be permitted.

3. Imperative is the reduction of the powers of the Public Service Commission, which are now so "extraordinarily broad" as to "increase the natural timidity of capital." At present (shameful to relate!) the commissioners "are under continuous pressure from associations of citizens and the public generally" and "corporations cannot anticipate the financial responsibilities that may be imposed on them."

4. "The fact that routes, service and fare may not be settled by considerations of financial return, but by the question of what may be best for the city at large, admits the logical conclusion that the city should make good any deficiency" "out of the annual tax budget." True, the constitution forbids public subsidies to private enterprises; but, surely, to make the subway "undertaking a safe business venture" constitutional obstacles can be overcome, and a "subsidy contract" entered into by which a private corporation shall build subways "provided the city shall contribute towards cost of operation such amount as shall be necessary to yield a certain net return upon the cost!"

"Heads I win; tails you lose." This is the only game which private capital will consent to play, says that high authority, the Chamber of Commerce.

Corporation money, then, is unavailable except on terms most unlikely to be accepted. Efforts to seduce corporation capital to relieve the situation merely waste time and postpone subway digging. And postponement is crime. Naturally the owners of the lines now in operation do not object to a postponement which means more strap-hanging. It is not their duty to consider the interests of the tenement dwellers who are left to swelter

---

* Report submitted March 4th, 1909.

in rack-rented flats. But a city official who condones postponement betrays his trust.

No Money for Subways?

There is no escape, even if escape were desirable. City money must be used again. How can it be raised? "Not by bond issues under the present law," say the city authorities. A grave indictment of themselves! Blind to the humane aspects of rapid transit and putting it in the class with sugar and dry-goods which private enterprise will furnish, they have lavished bond issues for other social purposes and have starved the most important social concern of all. During his administrations, says Mayor McClellan in his recent annual report, the total issue of corporate stock has been $298,945,000. Out of that immense sum how much has been authorized for rapid transit initiated by the administration? A beggarly $3,389,000. For the one service which is most vital to decent living, which increases taxable values and pays for itself besides, a picayune three millions! For this result social workers are, in part, responsible, since at their solicitation bonds have been freely issued for schools, parks, health and the like; while they have failed to urge the even greater social claims of rapid transit.

In October, 1908, according to the same report, the city had a margin of borrowing capacity of $44,333,556, more than enough to start a subway; but already that margin has been entrenched upon and still no allowance for transportation is mentioned.

By the Cassidy Committee a legal margin much wider was reported. The committee distinguished between legal debt and obligations resolved upon. Legally the bond issues already sanctioned and earmarked by the city for public works for which the contracts have not been actually signed do not constitute "debt"; but, by long-standing custom, in New York City they properly narrow the margin available for further enterprises. Conceivably the resolutions of the Board of Estimate and Apportionment could be rescinded and improvements agreed upon be abandoned up to the moment of signing contracts; but to depend for subway building upon such unusual action would be to lean upon a broken reed, unless, indeed, an administration be installed which is determined, before everything, to extend rapid transit.

By the tax valuations of 1909 the borrowing capacity of the city will be increased very little, for the final increase of real estate valuations, this year, on account of business depression, only about one hundred millions, may be largely offset by decreases in the special franchise assessments, following on the bankruptcy of the surface car lines and the lowered price of gas.

Under these circumstances, even if judicial investigation discloses a legal borrowing power of forty or fifty millions, it is unlikely that much of it can be reserved for subways, certainly not enough to meet the requirements.

Plainly, Father Knickerbocker is in a desperate strait. If sinister interests have sought to cripple him so that he can build himself no more transit lines they seem at first sight to have succeeded.

Two Ways to Finance the Lines.

But the city's extremity is the statesman's opportunity. Relief, on conditions as safe as a United States bond, can be won in two directions:

1. A constitutional amendment.
2. By assessing the cost of transit lines against the values they create.

A Constitutional Amendment.

A constitutional amendment providing that dock and transit bonds which are fully self-supporting need not be reckoned as debt has been sanctioned by one vote of the legislature because, as the Public Service Commission has said, "it is inconceivable that bonds for such enterprises should be considered a burden—rather they constitute an asset." If the constitutional amendment be sanctioned again in 1909 it will be submitted to a referendum vote in November and, being approved, the legislature in 1910 may pass laws providing "the method by which and the terms and conditions under which the amount of any debt to be so excluded (from reckonings as to the debt limit) shall be determined." And by the Appellate Division of the Supreme Court, subject to all the law's delays, may later be fixed, under that law, how much debt has been incurred for enterprises really self-supporting. Truly the precautions are ample!

Even if every step be taken as speedily as possible, not before 1911 will the money so freed become available, and the amount made available will depend upon the terms laid down by the legislature and the method of accounting adopted by the court. By that time conditions will be so intolerable that the curses of stifling tenement dwellers will justly fall on all who have obstructed this slow, long process of relief.

A vote for the constitutional amendment is a vote against higher rents and worse over-crowding.

One happy condition will attach to the funds so released. They cannot be used for any other purpose. An obstructive Board of Estimate might condemn them to lie idle; it could not dissipate them on less necessary works.

Profits to Land Owners From Subways.

But how inadequate to the situation even such aid will be! The Lexington-Broadway line alone—estimated to cost, with equipment, seventy-five millions, may absorb the funds liberated by the constitutional amendment for rapid transit and millions besides, in case, for example, the legislature should enact that liberated dock bonds shall not be used for subway construction. Further resources must also be tapped. Fortunately they lie at hand. By a painstaking investigation the City Club of New York has shown that, while the cost of the entire subway, without equipment, from the Battery to Spuyten Duyvil, was but $43,000,000 the rise in land values in Manhattan from 135th Street to the Spuyten Duyvil, and in the Bronx, due to the subway, after allowing generously for the full normal increase from general causes, was $80,500,000, up to 1907—and the end is not yet.

This territory could have paid out of its profits the whole cost of that part of the subway which runs through it and yet have cleared over $67,425,000.

These facts more than justify the remarks of the Public Service Commission that "there is much justice in the statement that the undeveloped or partly developed land in such localities should pay all or part of the cost of first construction." "No other class of public improvements has such a great, immediate and permanent effect upon land values as rapid transit lines, and this is particularly true of development route-lines running out into sparsely settled areas. (Precisely the case most promotive of social welfare.) This fact is extremely important for several reasons. In the first place, it makes this assessment less burdensome than others. Sewers, streets, parks, etc., may be laid out and assessed long before people find it possible to live in the newly-developed areas. As a result the owners must carry the assessment for a long period, or until they are able to sell to builders or to rent houses which they themselves may erect. But rapid transit lines bring people almost immediately, and often they are there before the lines are built. Further, the increase in values is much larger in proportion to the assessment than in many other lines. Consequently, the property-holders would be less opposed to the assessment and would have a larger profit after paying the assessment." In fact, "residents of localities now eagerly desiring rapid transit lines, realizing that these lines cannot be constructed . . . generally express themselves as willing to bear part of the burden."

Being human they would prefer to have the city continue the madly lavish policy of paying all the bills and giving the land-owners all the profits. But the city is like a drunkard who has tossed all his money among the crowd; its generosity is checked by want of means.

"By the methods advocated," continues the Public Service Commission, "funds to build the rapid transit line would be obtained by the sale of special assessment bonds which would not be a lien upon the city, but upon the property assessed."

Pay for the Lines out of Land Values They Create.

By a coincidence so striking as to seem providential this method possesses every advantage sought by rent-payers. It unites justice and economy with speed and ease of attainment and of all methods it best provides for low fares.

It is most just because it calls on those who take the profits also to pay the charges. Our city has been strangely blind to the modern mode of paying for costly transportation lines. Steam railways have long shown how to do it. When the traffic won't pay for the line the increase of land values created will fill the deficit. All but one of the transcontinental railways has been paid for in part by grants of lands, which, valueless before the line was built, enriched the railway treasuries within a few years of construction. Suburban trolley systems are often joined to schemes of real estate development to ensure dividends on the trolley lines. The Hudson Companies in New York have united vast land and development enterprises to their tunnel building to make it pay.

New York city cannot buy up acres of territory for development by subways, because it has neither the machinery nor the personnel requisite to make profits on the buying and selling of land. But it can enter into partnership with the owners, acting as their trustee and giving them the advantages of city powers. It can say to them: "You retain the land and take all the net profits. The city will build the line, giving you the services of the staff of the Public Service Commission, costing, for transit work, about $600,000 a year, free. You shall pay for the lines by instalments spread over a number of years, when your profits have materialized."

A Round Trip for a Nickel!

If the cost of construction be charged against the land-values created by the lines, fares need cover only the cost of equipment and operation, a fact which opens further rich possibilities of municipal improvement. Mr. Bion J. Arnold shows that a nickel fare on a future subway, built and equipped upon the latest designs, would yield a gross income of nineteen cents a car mile, while operating expenses and depreciation on the equipment would absorb 10.5 cents. Therefore a reduced fare would be practicable. A round-trip ticket for a nickel would yield 9.5 cents a car mile even if the travel were no heavier than with a fare of a nickel each way. But the increase of travel induced by the lower rate would probably bring up the car-mile earnings above 10.5 cents and yield a profit. A reduction of fare would be the proper reward for the district which had paid for the line, since lower fares would attract bigger crowds and make the rise of land values absolutely certain, thus richly rewarding the land-owners for their enterprise while offering better homes and lower rents to present tenement dwellers. Such an arrangement, agreed upon in advance between the city and the land-owners, should dissipate the fears of the timid owners and strengthen the resolution of the far-seeing.

It is seldom that a pitiless city problem admits of such an ideal solution, a solution which conserves all just interests, avoids all financial risks, satisfies the humane claims and demands no unusual ability for its application. By a combination of the rent-payers whom it would protect, the social workers whose duties it would lighten and the officials whose aim is the general good, the plan can be pushed to rapid consummation.

www.ingramcontent.com/pod-product-compliance
Lightning Source LLC
LaVergne TN
LVHW011147110826
845150LV00008B/2564